1 Introduction

Suicide is commended as an escape from the ills of life, and riches are to be despised. Aelian's Stoicism hardly goes below the surface. His primary object is to entertain and while so doing to convey instruction in the most agreeable form.

He was among the first to break away from the age-long tradition of the periodic structure of sentences, at least for works of a serious nature, and to affect a simpler prose of short, coordinated, sometimes paratactic, clauses.

In this and in the rich variety of topics and in a certain fondness for piquant, not to say earthy, stories from the life of men and of animals one may trace the infuence of the Milesian Tales.

Unfettered by any canons of style or language, picaresque, and sometimes gross, they pandered to popular taste. To adopt their technique while refining the style and imparting a moral favour to his narratives may well have seemed to Aelian a sure way of gaining a like popularity with educated readers.

Some might find fault with his random and piece-meal handling of his theme-of that he is well aware, and in the Epilogue he defends himself with the plea that a frequent change of topic helps to maintain the reader's interest and saves him from boredom.

But as to the permanent value of his work he has no misgivings, and since. Philostratus informs us that his writings were much admired, we may assume that they appealed to cultivated circles in a way that the voluminous and possibly arid compilations of grammarians did not.

2 The Ox and its services to man

Oxen are after all the most serviceable creatures. At sharing the farmer's labours, at carrying loads of various kinds, at filling the milk-pail — at all these things the Ox is excellent. He graces the altars, gladdens festivals, and provides a solemn banquet.

And even when dead the Ox is a splendid creature deserving our praise. At any rate bees are begotten of his carcase-bees, the most industrious of creatures, which afford the best and sweetest of fruits that man has, namely honey.

3 The Lion in Mauretania

A Lion will accompany a Moor on his journey and will drink water from the same spring. And I am told that Lions even resort to the houses of ' Moors when they fail to find any prey and are over- taken by the pangs of hunger.

And if the master of the house happens to be there, he keeps the Lion off and drives him away, pursuing him vigorously. If however he is out and his wife is left all alone, then with words that put the Lion to shame she checks his approach, restrains him, and admonishes him to control himself and not to allow his hunger to incense him.

The Lion, it seems, understands the Moorish tongue; and the sense of the rebuke which the woman administers to the animal is (so they say) as follows. 'Are not you ashamed, you, a Lion, the king of beasts, to come to my hut and to ask a Woman to feed you, and do you, like some cripple, look to a woman's hands hoping that thanks to her pity and compassion you may get what you want?

You who should be on your way to mountain haunts in pursuit of deer and antelopes and all other creatures that lions may eat without discredit. Whereas, like some sorry lap-dog, you are content to be fed by another. Such are the spells she employs, whereupon the Lion, as though his heart smote him and he were filled with shame, quietly and with downcast eyes moves off, overcome by the justice of her words.

Now if horses and hounds through being reared in their company understand and quail before the threats of men, I should not be surprised if Moors too, who are reared and brought up along with Lions, are understood by these very animals.

For the Moors profess to treat lion-cubs to the same kind of food, the same bed, and the same roof as their own children. Consequently there is nothing incredible or marvelous in Lions understanding human speech as described above.

4 The Horses of Libya

Concerning the Libyan Horse this is what I have learnt from accounts given by the Libyans. These Horses are exceedingly swift and know little or nothing of fatigue; they are slim and not well-feshed but are fitted to endure the scanty attention paid to them by their masters.

At any rate the masters devote no care to them: they neither rub them down nor roll them nor clean their hooves nor comb their manes nor plait their forelocks nor wash them when tired.

But as soon as they have completed the journey they intended they dismount and turn the Horses loose to graze. Moreover the Libyans themselves are slim and dirty, like the Horses which they ride.

Of Persia

The Persians on the other hand are proud and delicate, and what is more, their Horses are like them. One would say that both horse and master prided themselves on the size and beauty of their bodies and even on their finery and outward adornment.

5 Hounds of different countries

And here is a point which occurs to me to note in connexion with Hounds. The Cretan Hound is nimble and can leap and is brought up to range the mountains. Moreover the Cretans show the same qualities, such is the common report.
Among Hounds the Molossian is the most high-spirited, for the men also of Molossia are hot-tempered. In Carmania too both men .and Hounds are said to be most savage and implacable.

6 India devoid of pigs

The following also are examples of the peculiarities of animal nature. Ctesias reports that neither the wild nor the domestic Pig exists in India.

Its sheep

And he says somewhere that Indian Sheep have tails one cubit in Width.

The Ants of India

The Ants of India which guard the gold will not cross the river Campylinus. And the Issedonians who inhabit the same country as the Ants . . . they are called, and so they are.

Marjoram, antidote to snake poison

If a Tortoise eats part of a snake and thereafter some marjoram, it becomes immune from the poison which was bound to be quite fatal to it.

7 The Pigeon, its continence

I have heard people say that the Pigeon is of all birds the most temperate and restrained in its sexual relations.

For Pigeons never separate, neither the female bird unless by some mishap she is parted from her mate, nor the male unless he is widowed.

The Partridge, its incontinence

Partridges on the other hand are unrestrained in their indulgence. For that reason they destroy the eggs that have been laid, in order that the female birds may not be too busy with nursing their chicks to have time for sexual intercourse.

8 Wolves cross a river

When Wolves swim across a river Nature has devised for them an original safeguard to prevent them from being forcibly carried away by the impact of the stream and has taught them how to escape from difficulties, and that with ease.

Fastening their teeth in one another's tails they then breast the stream and swim across without harm or danger.

9 Animas antipathies

It is said that Nature has not bestowed the power of braying upon she-Asses. Nature too has enabled Hyenas to stop hounds from barking. The fragrance of perfumes causes death to Vultures; hemlock is the bane of Swans; Cyrus and Croesus learned how Horses dread camels, so the story goes.

Mares and foals

When Mares desert their foals and leave them, like orphans, before they are fully weaned, other Mares take compassion on them and bring them up with their own foals.

10 The Crow and Conjugal fidelity

Crows are exceedingly faithful to each other, and when they enter into partnership they love one another intensely, and you would never see these creatures indulging freely in promiscuous intercourse.

And those who are accurately informed about them assert that if one dies the other remains in widow-hood. I have heard too that men of old used actually at weddings to sing.

The Crow after the bridal song by way of pledging those who came together for the begetting of children to be of one mind. While those who observe the quarters from which birds come and their fight, declare that to hear a single Crow is an evil omen at a wedding.

Owl and Crow

Since the Owl is an enemy of the Crow and at night has designs upon the Crow's eggs, the Crow by day does the same to her, knowing that at that time the Owl's sight is feeble.

11 The Hedgehog

Nature has made the Hedgehog prudent and experienced in providing for its own wants. Thus, since it needs food to last a whole year, and since every season does not yield produce. It rolls among fig-crates (they say), and such dried figs as are pierced a great number become fixed upon its prickles-it quietly removes, and after laying up a store, keeps them and can draw from its nest when it is impossible to obtain food out of doors.

12 The Crocodile

It is a, fact that the fiercest of animals will, when the need arises, lay aside their natural savagery and be peaceful and gently disposed towards those that can be of service to them. For instance, the Crocodile swims with its jaws open; accordingly leeches fall into them and cause it pain.

And the Egyptian Plover

Knowing this it needs the Egyptian Plover as doctor. For when it is infested with leeches, it moves to the bank and opens its jaws to face the sun.

Whereupon the Egyptian Plover inserts its beak and draws out the aforesaid creatures, while the Crocodile endures this service and remains motionless.

So the bird gets a feast of leeches, while the Crocodile is benefited and reckons the fact that it has not injured it as the bird's fee.

13 The Jackdaw and Locusts

The inhabitants of Thessaly of Illyria and of Lemnos regard Jackdaws as benefactors and have decreed that they be fed at the public expense, seeing that Jackdaws make away with the eggs and destroy the young of the locusts which ruin the crops of the aforesaid people.

The clouds of locusts are in fact considerably reduced and the season's produce of these people remains undamaged.

14 Cranes and their migrations

Cranes have their birthplace in Thrace, which is the wintriest and the coldest region that I know of. Well, they love the country of their birth, but they love themselves too; so they devote part of their time to their ancestral haunts and part to their own preservation.

In summer they remain in their country, but in mid-autumn they leave for Egypt, Libya, and Ethiopia, appearing to know the map of the earth, the disposition of the winds, and the variations of the seasons.

And after spending a winter like spring, when again conditions are becoming tolerably settled and the sky is calm, they return. To lead their fight they appoint those that have already had experience of the journey; these would naturally be the older birds, and they select others of the same age to bring up the rear, while the young ones are ranged in their midst.

Having waited for a fair and favouring wind from behind, and using it as an escort to speed them forward, they then form their order of fight into an acute-angled triangle, in order that as they encounter the air they may cleave it with the least difficulty, and so hold on their way.

This then is how Cranes spend their summer and winter. (But mankind regards. as marvelous the Persian king's comprehension of temperature, and harps on Susa and Ecbatana and the repeated stories of the Persian's journeying to and fro.)

When however the Cranes observe an eagle bearing down upon them, they form a circle and in a bellying mass threaten him with attack; and he retires. Resting their bills upon each other's tail-feathers they form in a sense a continuous chain of fight, and sweeten their labour as they repose gently one upon another.

And in some distant land . . . when they light upon some water-spring they rest for the night and sleep, while three or four mount guard for all the others; and in order to avoid falling asleep during their watch they stand on one leg, but with the other held up the clutch a stone firmly and securely in their claws.

Their object is that, if they should inadvertently drop off to sleep, the stone should fall and wake them with the sound. Now the stone which a Crane swallows to give itself ballast is a touchstone for gold when regurgitated by the Crane after it has, so to say, come to anchor and reached land.

Cranes give warning of storms

If a pilot observes on the high seas a flock of Cranes turning and flying back, he realizes that they have refrained from advancing further owing to the assault of a contrary wind.

And taught, as you might say, by the birds he sails home again and preserves his vessel. So the pilot's art, being a lesson and a discipline first acquired by these birds, has been handed on to mankind.

15 The Pigeon

In cities Pigeons congregate with human beings; they are
extremely tame and swarm about one's feet; but in lonely
places they fee away and cannot endure human beings.
For it is crowds that give them courage, and they are well
aware that they will be unmolested. Where however there are
bird-catchers, nets, and schemes to take them.
They dwell' no more 'without fear,' to quote what Euripides
says of those same birds.

16 The Partridge and its nest

When Partridges are about to lay they make themselves what is called a ' threshing-foor' (i.e. nest) out of dry twigs. It is plaited, hollow, and well- suited for sitting in. They pour in dust and construct as it were a soft bed.

They enter and after screening themselves over with dry twigs so as to avoid being seen by birds of prey and by human hunters, they lay their eggs in complete tranquility. Next, they do not entrust their eggs to the same place but to some other, emigrating as it were, because they are afraid that they may perhaps be detected.

And when they hatch their young they impart heat to them, being callow, and warm them with their wings, enveloping them in their feathers, as it might be swaddling-clothes. They do not however wash them, but render them more sleek by putting dust on them.

And its young

If a Partridge sees someone approaching with evil intent against itself and its young, it thereupon rolls about in front of, the hunter's feet and fills him with the hope of seizing it as it moves this way and that.

And the man bends down to catch his prey, but it eludes him. Meantime the young ones slip away and get some distance ahead. So when the Partridge is aware of this, it takes courage and releases the bird- catcher from his fruitless occupation by flying off, leaving the man gaping.

Then when the mother- bird is secure and advantageously placed, she calls her chicks, and they recognising her voice flutter towards her.

The male bird

The Partridge when about to lay her eggs endeavors to hide from her mate for fear that he may crush them, because he is lustful and tries to prevent the mother from devoting her time to rearing her young, So incontinent a creature is the Partridge.

When the females leave the males and brood their eggs, the male birds of set purpose provoke one another to anger and deal and receive the most violent blows; and the vanquished bird gets trodden, the victor performing unsparingly, until he in his turn is vanquished and is caught in like clutches.

17 Jealousy in certain animals

Euripides says that jealousy is an accursed thing. It seems that there are certain animals in which this quality resides. For instance, the Gecko, according to Theophrastus when it has sloughed its skin, turns and makes away with it by swallowing it.

It seems that the slough of this creature is a remedy for epilepsy. And the Deer too, knowing that its right horn serves many purposes, goes so far as to bury it and secrete it out of jealousy lest anyone should benefit thereby.

The Mare also knows that with the birth of a foal she is producing love-spells; and that is why the moment the foal is born, the Mare bites of the piece of flesh on its forehead. Men call it mare's frenzy.

And wizards maintain that such things produce and excite impulses to unrestrained sexual intercourse and a lecherous passion. So the Mare does not wish men to have any of this spell, as though she grudged them a boon beyond compare. And is it not so?

Get All The Books In The Series:

www.ingramcontent.com/pod-product-compliance
Lightning Source LLC
Chambersburg PA
CBHW050926290526
45792CB00002B/908